JOBS IN OUR COMMUNITY

TEACHERS

on the Job

By David Anthony

KidHaven
PUBLISHING

Published in 2017 by
KidHaven Publishing, an Imprint of Greenhaven Publishing, LLC
353 3rd Avenue
Suite 255
New York, NY 10010

Designer: Deanna Paternostro
Editor: Katie Kawa

Photo credits: Cover wizdata/Shutterstock.com; p. 5 Brocreative/Shutterstock.com; p. 7 Pressmaster/ Shutterstock.com; pp. 9, 19 wavebreakmedia/Shutterstock.com; p. 11 Andresr/ Shutterstock.com; p. 13 michaeljung/iStock/Thinkstock; p. 15 Monkey Business Images/Monkey Business/Thinkstock; p. 17 Digital Vision/Photodisc/Thinkstock; p. 21 omgimages/iStock/Thinkstock; p. 23 monkeybusinessimages/iStock/Thinkstock.

Cataloging-in-Publication Data

Names: Anthony, David.
Title: Teachers on the job / David Anthony.
Description: New York : KidHaven Publishing, 2017. | Series: Jobs in our community| Includes index.
Identifiers: ISBN 9781534521605 (pbk.) | ISBN 9781534521476 (library bound) | ISBN 9781534521469 (6 pack) | ISBN 9781534521483 (ebook)
Subjects: LCSH: Teachers–Juvenile literature.
Classification: LCC LB1775.A548 2017 | DDC 371.1–dc23

Printed in the United States of America

CPSIA compliance information: Batch #CW17KL: For further information contact Greenhaven Publishing LLC, New York, New York at 1-844-317-7404.

Please visit our website, www.greenhavenpublishing.com. For a free color catalog of all our high-quality books, call toll free 1-844-317-7404 or fax 1-844-317-7405.

CONTENTS

School is fun! You
go to school to learn
with your friends.

Teachers work at a school. They help their **students** learn.

Most teachers have their own classroom full of students.

Teachers help students use a **computer**.

11

Teachers show their students how to write letters and numbers.

12

Kids learn to read at school, too. Teachers read stories to their students.

Teachers answer questions their students have. Teachers ask questions, too.

Some teachers are art teachers. They help kids draw and paint.

Music teachers help their students play **instruments.** They teach kids new songs.

Teachers work hard
to make school fun!

WORDS TO KNOW

computer

instruments

students

INDEX